You Arrested Me for What?

You Arrested Me for What?

A Bail Bondsman's Observations
of Virginia's Criminal Justice System

Dan Barto

Edited by Linda Gardner
Interior and cover design by Steve Amarillo
Cover illustration by Dan Johnson
Logo illustration by Quinn Barto
Logo art digitized by Jim Crantas

Dan Barto Publishing
www.thebondsmanVA.com

ISBN 978-0-692-54490-7

10 9 8 7 6 5 4 3 2 1
Printed in the United States of America

Contents

Contents

Introduction

My name is Dan Barto. Professionally, I've been a software developer for over twenty years. When I was closing in on age fifty, it occurred to me that, should I lose my job, I didn't have anything to fall back on. I felt I needed to get something going. I started researching a possible second profession. One thing led to another, and I fell into writing bail bonds. For anyone who doesn't know what bondsmen do, we get people out of jail while they wait for their trial.

For the most part, I've been a law-abiding citizen, so my experience with the laws was minimal. Performing this job has made me much more aware of how our judicial system in Virginia, at least a portion of it, operates.

There are many things our criminal justice system does right. However, I see some of the inadequacies, and sometimes injustices, of our system and the negative effect they have on people's everyday lives. I found, while talking with people who go through the judicial system, whether justly or unjustly, that they are passionate about the injustice of unnecessary burdens our state and local judicial systems put on people. This is especially true for the younger adults.

After becoming aware of these issues, the impetus for this book was born. It came to me that I should write my observations of our justice system in Virginia, good or bad. Hopefully, this book will at least create a discussion among Virginians and bring about changes in some of the questionable laws and practices.

Chapter One

What Is Bail Bonding, and How Does It Work?

It is important to understand the basics of bail bonding—what it is and how it works in a nutshell. Simply put, the bail system is a way for the court to obtain a guarantee that a defendant will show up at his or her court proceedings. It allows defendants to be released from jail and continue their lives while awaiting trial, which alleviates overcrowding in the jails.

When someone is arrested, that person is typically taken to a local jail for booking. During the booking process, a magistrate will decide whether or not to set bail. Once arrested and booked, the magistrate will evaluate the defendant and the circumstances, and then either set a bond, allow the defendant to be released, or have the defendant remain in jail without bond until the defendant appears before a judge.

If a bond is set, the defendant's loved ones have a few options to get him or her out of jail. If the defendant's family or friends are financially capable and willing, the full amount of the bond can be paid, in cash, to the magistrate. Then, after the defendant fulfills all court appearances, the entire amount is refunded. The obvious advantage of this is that it ends up costing nothing to get out of jail.

Depending on the jail, a second option may be to use the title of an automobile or the mortgage of a house or other property as collateral to the court. A lien will be placed on the title, or property, while the defendant awaits trial. Once all court proceedings are finalized, the lien is released. If the defendant flees, the automobile or property is then in jeopardy. However, many of the Virginia jurisdictions don't provide this option.

The last method is for the defendant's loved ones to hire a bail bondsman to execute the bond for the defendant's release. The bail bond agent is contacted by the friend or family member for the initial consultation. This consultation involves gathering basic information about the defendant and cosigner(s), allowing the bail agent to assess the risk of posting the bond for the defendant. The agent will also inform the person of the cost of the bond premium, usually 10 percent of the bond amount plus a processing fee, required to bail out the defendant.

When both parties are satisfied with the conditions of the release, they will, typically, meet at the jail where the defendant is held. Once there, payment will be made and paperwork will be filled out and signed. The bond is then posted, and the defendant is released from jail.

Chapter Two

Bail Bonding Business:
Past and Present

Once I had decided to pursue becoming a bondsman, I took the bail bondsman class, passed the state property and casualty insurance exam, and applied to the appropriate state agencies. The last step was to find a bonding agency to hire me to write bail bonds.

So I started making phone calls to local and regional bail bondsmen. Honestly, it didn't take that many rejections, less than ten, before I connected with a bondsman who talked to me and was genuinely interested in taking on a bondsman. Fortunately, he turned out to be an honest guy and it worked out.

However, the rejections are the point of this; not because I have a delicate ego and my feelings were hurt. They weren't. It was because of the consistency of what the bondsmen said. A typical conversation was as follows:

"Hi. My name is Dan Barto. I'll be a newly licensed bondsman shortly, and I'm looking for someone to hire me to write bail bonds. Would you be interested in having another agent write for you?"

"Do you already have a job?" would be the response.

"Yes," I replied.

"Good. Keep it. This industry sucks. It used to be good, but pretrial services and a flood of new bondsmen ruined it. You'll regret becoming a bondsman."

Click.

After a few of those types of conversations, the thought did cross my mind that I had made a mistake. Still, I went forward with it, and, thus far, it has worked out.

After being in this business and interacting with other bondsmen, that sentiment is the norm, at least among the more seasoned bonding agents. Any bondsman who has been around for over ten years will say that the boom years are over. There are fewer bonds to write and more competition to get them. However, the biggest complaint among bonding agents is pretrial services.

In a nutshell, pretrial services performs several tasks for the court. Aside from helping the defendants get out of jail, pretrial services compiles reports on defendants to assist the judiciary for release and detention decisions. Once defendants are released, pretrial services may monitor them to enforce the compliance to the conditions of the court. Pretrial services is covered in more detail in the following chapter. However, for this topic, just keep in mind the following: first, the original stated goal of pretrial services was to provide help only to the indigent (those who have no means to get a bail bond executed). Second, once pretrial services gets a case, that defendant is removed from the bail bonding pool of potential clients, and third and most importantly, when a defendant is assigned to report to pretrial services as a condition of the bond, they're essentially on parole before being found guilty.

Chapter Three

Pretrial Services: What Is It, and What Is Its Value?

Pretrial services and commercial bail bonding go together like oil and water. It has been like that since the inception of pretrial services, back in the 1960s. To understand this relationship, it's important to first go through the history of pretrial services in America.

Before getting into it, there is an admission to be made. This topic is somewhat policy-heavy. If you've got any type of interest or stake in pretrial services or bail bonding, hopefully you'll find this section interesting and get something out of it. Otherwise, I would suggest reading, at a minimum, the "The Fundamental Flaw with Virginia's Pretrial Services" (chapter 5) and the "Bottom Line" section at the end of chapter 7.

History of Pretrial Services

The bail reform movement started in New York in the early 1960s with a study conducted by the Vera Institute of Justice. The study, which was created as a response to the injustice of the legal system for lower income people and became known as the Manhattan Bail Project, found (1) many defendants remained in jail because they couldn't afford the bond, and (2) local people with strong ties were unlikely to skip bond.

In 1963, then-Attorney General Robert Kennedy formed a committee that issued a report focused on bail and detainment for the poor. In 1968, Washington DC created the first pretrial services program. It went beyond its original stated mission of arranging for bail bonds for the indigent and began the additional tasks of collecting and verifying defendant information, producing reports and recommendations, and supervising the defendants.

With DC pioneering the way, pretrial release programs have assumed a larger role in jurisdictions, evolving into comprehensive programs charged with monitoring the entire system of release. Pretrial services programs are the first criminal justice system players to assess and identify the needs of a defendant. They are also the gatekeepers for alternative placements. Pretrial programs gather and verify information about the accused (criminal history, status in the criminal justice system, address, employment, and drug or alcohol use). Pretrial programs also assess defendants' likelihood for failure to appear (FTA) at court proceedings or for rearrest while on release. Pretrial services programs present the judge with this information, allowing him or her to use it in determining appropriate pretrial release/detention and conditions. Once the judge reaches his decision, the pretrial programs then function as the supervisors of the defendants on release and notify the courts upon any violation of release conditions.[1]

Pretrial services continued to move forward at the federal level with the Bail Reform Act of 1966, which created a presumption of release. It also required the court to be as lenient as possible with pretrial conditions, as long as there was reasonable assurance the defendant would return for all future court commitments. Congress then passed the pretrial services act of 1982, which authorized the establishment of pretrial services in all judicial districts, save the District of Columbia.

States soon began adopting pretrial services. In 1995, Virginia passed the Comprehensive Community Corrections Act and the Pretrial Services Act (§ 19.2-152.2 of the Virginia Code), authorizing pretrial services by statute. Authorized by the Department of Criminal Justice Services (DCJS), state funds would be offered to the counties and cities to create and maintain programs "for the purpose of providing the judicial system with sentencing alternatives to offenders convicted of certain misdemeanors and nonviolent felonies, pretrial background investigations, and supervision for pretrial defendants."[2] The responsibilities of the pretrial services officers have been codified in the Virginia Code §19.2-152.4:3.

Since then, most Virginia cities and counties have adopted pretrial services into their court system. As of 2013, there were "currently 31 pretrial services agencies in Virginia, providing services in 97 of the 133 localities in the Commonwealth."[3]

Chapter Four

The Rift between Pretrial Services and Commercial Bail

It is easy to see why the bail bonding industry does not like pretrial services: they're horning in on the bail bondsmen's turf and reducing demand for their services. You might be thinking, "Well, it's those greedy bondsmen who just want to make more money." That is really just a cynical characterization, and it completely ignores the agenda of many in the pretrial services industry.

Keep in mind, the original stated goal of pretrial services was to provide a means for the indigent to be released from jail while awaiting trial. That's a pretty good idea. For someone who is down on their luck with no family, their only option was to sit in jail and await trial. However, pretrial services has become much more than that. It's a government agency. Like most government agencies, it gets bigger, more bureaucratic, and inevitably takes on a life of its own, oftentimes extending its duties far beyond the original intent. It's no secret that it has become an agenda of the pretrial services lobby to completely abolish commercial bail bonding.

As an example of this agenda, here's an excerpt from a 2012 article from the Justice Policy Institute:

> Every jurisdiction should follow the lead of the four states where for-profit bail bonding is banned and institute robust, risk-based pretrial programs. . . . While pursuing

the elimination of for-profit bail bonding, jurisdictions should implement guidelines and procedures that promote non-financial release.[4]

Unfortunately, that's not untypical of those in leadership roles in the pretrial services industry. Here's another from the *Baltimore Sun* in 2013 where the task force recommends "scrapping" the bail system:

> In recommendations released this week, task force members said the state should scrap the system under which poor defendants often remain in jail while more affluent suspects can post bond and get out.[5]

Also, the National Association of Pretrial Services Agencies (NAPSA) has long been calling for an end to the private bail system, and they are very clear about it. In the 2004 NAPSA Pretrial Standards for Virginia, they call for all compensated sureties to be abolished.[6]

So it's clear the goal is to eliminate commercial bail bonding entirely, and they're not trying to hide it. One doesn't have to speculate how bail would work if commercial bail bonding ceased to exist, since there are already four states that have banned it—Oregon, Kentucky, Illinois, and Wisconsin have banned commercial bail.

So what happens if someone is arrested and given a bond? To get someone bonded out of jail, the entire 10 percent has to be paid up front, along with processing fees, which can range from $25 to $75. Depending on the jurisdiction, it can be paid either at the court, jail, or sheriff's office. If the arrestee attends all of his or her court dates, the 10 percent minus the court fees and the fees for a court-appointed lawyer, if used, are deducted. What this really means is the 10 percent is essentially the prepayment for the court costs if all court appearances are attended by the defendant. So what happens when someone skips bond? That person is then a fugitive who is indebted to the court for the full amount of the bond; they forfeit the 10 percent and will also have to pay court costs.

Chapter Five

The Fundamental Flaw with Virginia's Pretrial Services

A fundamental principle of our criminal justice process is that a defendant is innocent until proven guilty. I maintain that a bulk of what pretrial services does in Virginia is in violation of that very principle. A defendant going through pretrial services is not unlike a convicted offender going through probation. Going through pretrial services is essentially being sentenced to probation prior to being tried and found guilty.

When someone is arrested, tried, and found guilty, he or she may be given a probationary period to go through as part of the consequences. What exactly is probation? A typical definition reads as follows:

> Probation is the suspension of a jail sentence that allows a person convicted of a crime a chance to remain in the community, instead of going to jail. Probation requires that you follow certain court-ordered rules and conditions under the supervision of a probation officer. Typical conditions may include performing community service, meeting with your probation officer, refraining from using illegal drugs or excessive alcohol, avoiding certain people and places, and appearing in court during requested times.[7]

In short, if given probation, a convicted person has to check in with the probation officer periodically and may have to meet other conditions. If the offender does not adhere to the conditions, a capias, or an order to arrest, may be issued against the offender. If this occurs, the offender will be rearrested with a probation violation charge.

This process, through pretrial services, is very similar to being sentenced to probation. After someone is arrested, the first appearance before the judge is the arraignment. There, a judge may order the defendant to report to pretrial services as a condition of the bond. The defendant will then be required to report to a pretrial services agent, usually once a week, where he or she is supervised by the agent. The defendant may also be required to submit to drug testing or to attend education or treatment programs. Like probation, pretrial services can issue a capias against the defendant for failure to comply with the stated conditions, in which case the defendant (who has not yet been found guilty) will incur another charge.

For example, suppose a defendant is charged with drug possession, and the judge requires the defendant to report to pretrial services for drug testing and treatment. While awaiting trial and out on bond, the defendant has to report to pretrial services, where he or she will be drug tested. The defendant will also have to attend a drug treatment class. Now suppose the defendant misses a pretrial services date and/or fails a drug test and is rearrested and charged with an additional offense, and another bond is issued for the defendant to be released from jail. Later, at the trial, the original drug charge is dismissed. Now the defendant has the resulting charge to resolve, which came about from an apparently bogus drug charge.

On its face, this is not right. When defendants are out on bond awaiting trial, they shouldn't be placed in a probationary lifestyle, which is exactly what pretrial services is. While there may be some nuanced differences between pretrial services and probation, like rules, guidelines, etc., the biggest, glaring, elephant-in-the-room difference is that probation is done after someone is tried and found guilty, while pretrial services is for the defendant who is awaiting trial. From the defendant's perspective, they're essentially the same: one is prior to the trial while the other is after being found guilty.

Many regard this function of pretrial services as a way to set the defendant up to fail. For instance, suppose the defendant has a serious drug addiction. By putting that person in pretrial services to be drug tested, the odds are pretty good the defendant will fail a drug test somewhere in the process. When that happens, the defendant goes back to jail to deal with the additional charge and will have to pay more costs, such as court fees, to the court.

I have spoken with many of my clients about their experience with pretrial services. Some have said the agent who was assigned to them was pretty good, while others expressed contempt for the assigned agent as well as the entire process. While awaiting trial and assigned to pretrial services, one of my clients was having fairly serious health issues. Because of this, she was unable to check in. However, both she and her lawyer made numerous attempts to contact her pretrial services agent by leaving messages. Their voice messages were never returned. The pretrial services agent twice issued capiases on my client, and twice they were dismissed when my client brought in her phone records to prove all reasonable attempts had been made to contact pretrial services. While these charges were ultimately dismissed, they were a burden to have to deal with for my client. This scenario should not have happened at all.

In addition, the notion of forcing the defendant to show up once a week during the workday can be beyond burdensome and inconvenient. Depending on someone's employment, locality, or inaccessibility to transportation, the defendant can have a very difficult time keeping these appointments. I've had clients who work thirty miles away and have to take off work to check in with their pretrial services agent. Is this not a form of punishment? Now suppose it was a bogus charge and it gets dismissed at the trial. The court forced the defendant to miss work, lose pay, and spend gas money each week to visit pretrial services for a bogus charge. Can that person be blamed for having contempt for their local government?

The burden and stress of just having to meet with pretrial services weekly is disproportionally difficult on the poor and working poor. For people who are just barely scraping by, to require them to meet with their agent weekly can be almost impossible to accomplish without some degree of failure. I had one client who lived on the south side of Richmond and had to attend Henrico pretrial services, which is approximately ten to twelve miles each way. She was an unemployed single mother and didn't have a car and certainly couldn't afford a cab, so she had to bum rides from family and friends each week. Care to place odds on her missing a pretrial services appointment? Did I mention that many people believe pretrial services are set up to make people fail?

One of the purposes of the bail system is to allow the defendants to continue to live their lives while awaiting trial. This implementation of pretrial services undermines that and should be stopped. It's simply wrong.

Chapter Six

Pretrial Services vs. Commercial Bail: Compare and Contrast

Putting aside that pretrial services foists undo punishment and consequences upon defendants prior to being found guilty, let's compare and contrast commercial bail to pretrial services in terms of efficiency, cost, and the practical aspects of each. I maintain that the advantages commercial bail has over pretrial services are: (1) it provides a stronger motivation for the defendant to appear for all court dates; (2) when a defendant does refuse to go to court, they'll more likely be recovered; (3) costs to the taxpayer are much less; and (4) corruption is minimized.

In explaining the first advantage of defendants being less likely to miss court when bonded out by a bail bondsman, it's important to emphasize a particular step in how commercial bail bonds are executed. That step is having a cosigner to the bond being financially responsible for the entire amount of the bond. Most often, it's a family member. This puts added pressure for the defendant to go to court. If the court date is missed, the family member (cosigner) loses his/her money. That consequence does not exist with pretrial services.

As an example of this, I recall one of my clients who had skipped court and initially had no intention of going back to court. I had bonded him out on a $2,500 bond for a Schedule I or II drug charge, which means a felony drug, such as heroin or cocaine. Understand that drug addicts are among the riskiest bonds to write because, if they're really hooked and not committed to staying clean, nothing seems to take precedence over their next fix. Additionally, they know that if they go back to jail, they're going cold turkey, which is a strong motivation to do anything to avoid jail. Anyhow, this defendant's brother cosigned for him. I recall discussing the repercussions with the brother, explaining to him how risky it was. He assured me that he would make sure his brother would show up to court. Further, the defendant's brother proved to have a stable, semi-lucrative job and could cover the $2,500 should his brother skip court. To make a long story short, I executed the bond and he skipped court. I found this out in the morning, a couple of days after the court date and immediately called the brother and left a message on his voicemail. Later that same day, the brother called me back. To my surprise, he said that his brother had already turned himself in. I verified this to be true. When I asked what had happened, he said had been been out of town on business for the last couple of weeks. He hadn't been able to contact his brother, so he contacted their mutual friends. When he found out the court appearance had been missed, he told the friends to let his brother know that he was coming home. If he hadn't turned himself in by the time his brother got back to Richmond, his brother was going to "kick his ass." That is why he turned himself in.

This type of situation would never happen with pretrial services, because no one is on the hook except the taxpayer. Admittedly, this is not typical of most skips. What is typical is the cosigner of a bond telling me that should the person being bonded out skip, they will kill them. This is the strongest advantage commercial bail bonds have over pretrial services. There is a personal connection between the cosigner, who is financially responsible for the bond, the bondee, who got bonded out of jail, and the bondsman. When someone is bonded out with pretrial services, no one has real skin in the game except the defendant. If the defendant skips, the pretrial services persons aren't responsible. There is no cosigner. No one is responsible; therefore, no one pays (directly). Furthermore, that defendant, who is now a fugitive, will likely take up more resources from police and sheriff departments, as well as the court systems.

Regarding the second advantage of getting a fugitive back into court, the advantage the commercial bondsman has is having established personal contacts with the defendant. The fact that money is at stake for the cosigner and the bondsman is a big motivator to return the fugitive to court and get off of the bond. There are real consequences for people involved in the case. Again, that doesn't exist with pretrial services.

The third advantage is cost. Who pays for this? With commercial bail, it's the people who are using the services. With pretrial services, it's the local and state governments, so it falls on the Virginia taxpayer.

The fourth advantage of less corruption has to do with the alternative to commercial bail. Suppose commercial bail is shut down. What is the replacement? There would still be bonds, and when someone is given a bond, there would still be the 10 percent cost to get out. So who gets the 10 percent premium? The court does until the case is closed. If the defendant attends all court dates, the 10 percent premium is first used to pay court fees, with the remainder, if there is a remainder, being returned to the defendant. If the defendant misses court, the 10 percent is not returned, plus the defendant has to pay the full amount of the bond. It would be another revenue generator for the state and local justice agencies. Should the state be trusted with this? Suppose the local government is in need of more funds and it collects the 10 percent fee for all bail bonds. Might that be a temptation to increase the cost of the bond, or issue bail bonds that aren't needed, or both? I am convinced it would. With commercial bail, the government gets none of the 10 percent fee, so there's no incentive for the state to issue more bonds at a higher cost.

Now what about corrupt bail bondsmen? There are admittedly some bad bondsmen, but most bondsmen are not. It's no different than most any other industry. Are there crooked plumbers or lousy teachers? Yes, but that doesn't mean they're all bad. In Virginia, the bail bonding industry is regulated by the Virginia Department of

Criminal Justice Services (DCJS). There can be repercussions against corrupt bondsmen, and there should be. The big point here is it's easier to fix an issue with a bad bondsman than it is to undo a bad judicial process. If a bondsman is found to be corrupt, this can be quickly remedied by taking away his or her license. On the other hand, what if an agency, judge, or bureaucratic process is corrupt? How are any of those remedied? Most of them are not.

A further point is that the DCJS should enforce the regulations that are on the books. A common complaint I hear from other bondsmen is that the DCJS does not enforce their rules.

As an example, Virginia Code sections 9.1-185.9 and 9.1-185.12 read:

> § 9.1-185.9. Solicitation of business; standards; restrictions and requirements.
>
> A. Only licensed bail bondsmen shall be authorized to solicit bail bond business in the Commonwealth.
>
> B. *A licensed bail bondsman shall not:*
>> *1. Solicit bail bond business by directly initiating contact with any person in any court, jail, lock-up, or surrounding government property.*
>>
>> *2. Loiter by any jail or magistrate's office unless there on legitimate business.*
>
> § 9.1-185.12. Uniforms and identification; standards and restrictions.
>
> A. A bail bondsman shall not wear, carry, or display any uniform, badge, shield, or other insignia or emblem that implies he is an agent of state, local, or federal government.
>
> B. *A bail bondsman shall wear or display only identification issued by, or whose design has been approved by, the Department.*

[Emphasis added]

I recall being in the Norfolk General District Court building and seeing a bail bondsman in the hallway holding up a sign that said "Bail Bonds." There are also complaints of bondsmen who loiter at the jails and solicit bonds as people walk into the magistrate's office. Many times, bondsmen have told me they have filed complaints with DCJS, but action is rarely taken. Honest bondsmen cheer seeing the corrupt bondsmen punished for unethical practices. It would be better to improve the DCJS process for better enforcement of their rules, rather than implicating and throwing the entire bail industry under the bus (unless there's another agenda at play).

Chapter Seven

What Makes Pretrial Services Bad?

In a perfect criminal justice world, pretrial services' role would be, at most, to process the indigent, as was the original stated goal. As already detailed, it has now morphed into an immoral sentencing practice, where defendants are forced into probationary consequences as if already found guilty.

Aside from that, what else is wrong with pretrial services? While most people working in pretrial services agencies may be decent, law-abiding citizens who are just trying to do their job well, what makes pretrial services bad are the people and organizations leading it. To best show this, I decided to take a prominent pretrial services organization and address their arguments for getting rid of commercial bail. As stated before, the pretrial services lobby's agenda is to eradicate commercial bail. So what are their arguments for doing this? Are their criticisms of commercial bail valid? Are they intellectually honest or are they dishonest? I believe I can show that their arguments for getting rid of commercial bail don't hold up to scrutiny.

The organization looked at is the Justice Policy Institute (JPI). It's a Washington DC based nonprofit organization with the mission statement, "JPI is dedicated to reducing use of incarceration and the justice system by promoting fair and effective policies."[8] Note: their mission statement alone, by using vague and misleading words like "fair" and "effective," should raise a red flag. Everyone wants policies to be fair. But what is fair to one person is quite possibly unfair to the next. Groups and people who throw that word around usually mean, "If you don't agree with me, then you're unfair."

In September of 2012, The Justice Policy Institute published a forty-seven-page article titled "For Better or For Profit: How the Bail Bonding Industry Stands in the Way of Fair and Effective Pretrial Justice."[9] It was written by Spike Bradford. The title states the gist of the article.

Before getting into their specific arguments, the terminology used by JPI has to be addressed. Words have meanings and when carefully chosen can elicit an impression. For example, rather than calling a frog a "frog," calling it a "slimy, green, slothful creature" characterizes the frog in a way that gives a negative impression of the frog. This is what Bradford has done with commercial bail. Rather than calling it "commercial bail," it's referred to as "for profit." In its glossary, it has definitions for "for-profit bail bondsman" and for "for-profit bail industry." This is likely intended to give a negative impression of bail bondsmen as being all about money with no regard for the people with whom they are dealing. So be it, but to put this on an equal playing field, there should also be a characterization for pretrial services.

With that in mind, pretrial services programs in this book will now be referred to as "government-worker bail." Yes, I'll be transparent and honest and acknowledge that this is to elicit an impression of an inefficient, uncaring, can't-be-fired, government worker. They're very much like the stereotype of what you deal with when going to the DMV, except the bail bond government worker might make you pee in a cup. So the alternatives are not "commercial bail" versus "pretrial services," but rather "for-profit bail" versus "government-worker bail."

So with that stated, here are my responses to the JPI criticisms of "for-profit bail":

Bail Bondsmen Are Taking Advantage of Low Income Communities

Government-worker bail maintains that because bail bondsmen charge 10 percent (which is mandated by the state), we're taking advantage of the lower and middle class people. JPI claims bondsmen actually have no risk, because they have a legal contract with the cosigners and can obtain the cosigners' assets at any time, and they always get their money. Bradford's article states:

> The bail bonding industry justifies retention of the full fee as compensation for the risks they take and costs they accrue. However, this risk appears to be overstated on two counts. First, those who pay the fee for the bond have signed a legal contract. Bail bondsmen don't write contracts to bail someone out unless they have evidence that the co-signers have the resources to pay. Whether it's a ranch in Montana or a car repair shop in Maryland, the bail bondsman can legally take the assets of co-signers if the defendant doesn't make their court appearance and the bail is forfeited.[10]

This statement alone tells me that the author, Spike Bradford, appears to have spent very little time, if any, consulting actual bail bondsmen. Or maybe he consulted them, but just decided to disregard the feedback he received. Either way, the above statement is not accurate at all. He maintains that the risks that for-profit bail assumes are largely overstated because bondsmen have cosigners and can get the money from the cosigner(s).

It is true that bondsmen do have cosigners who are legally and financially responsible for the bail bond. However, when a defendant skips court, the court will come after the bondsman for the full amount of the bond. First, should the cosigner refuse to pay, the bondsman must decide whether or not to proceed to civil court. There are court fees and expenses to this. Note also that even if the bondsman is awarded compensation, that does not guarantee the cosigner pays. There may be an option of wage garnishment, but that is another process to go through with more expenses associated with it as well as exceptions to it. For example, disability payments cannot be garnished. And good luck getting money out of the Montana ranch!

So when Bradford asserts that for-profit bail takes advantage of low-income people and assumes little risk, he's simply wrong.

Where Does the Money Go?

Bradford has a page that shows the options for bail that charts to whom the money is paid. He lists four options for bail: a cash bail, a recognizance bond, a government-worker bail (which is referred to as a deposit bail), and a for-profit bail (which is referred to as for-profit bail).[11] Since neither a cash bail bond nor a recognizance bond requires any outside assistance from bondsmen or government workers, I will compare the government-worker bail to for-profit bail with an example of a person arrested and given a $2,000 bond.

First, with government-worker bail, the defendant, or a friend or loved one, would pay the $200 premium to the jail, sheriff's office, or court. There are also fees involved, which do not get refunded. A $2,000 bond will cost between $225 and $275. If the defendant attends all of the assigned court dates, the $200 is refunded, less court fees and other costs. Should the defendant fail to appear, the $200 is not returned, and $2,000 is then owed to the court by the defendant. So when the government-worker bail lobby maintains that pretrial services removes the bail money barrier for the poor, it is simply not true, because the defendant must still pay the 10 percent, plus the fee, to get out of jail in the first place. It is even more deceptive to say the 10 percent is returned. Court fees and fines are paid first with the 10 percent, so the 10 percent bail premium which the defendant *must* pay prior to getting out is a down payment to the court for court costs, fees, and fines.

With for-profit bail, the family would pay $200 to the bonds-man. Most bondsmen do charge a fee as well, typically anywhere between $25 and $50. Regardless of whether the defendant attends all assigned court dates or fails to appear, that $200 premium is not returned. Should the defendant skip court, the $2,000 is then owed to the bondsman.

Again, recall that the initial goal of pretrial services was to provide the service to the indigent. If someone has no means of payment, they shouldn't have to sit in jail awaiting their court date if they are deemed a low flight risk. I have no problem with that. It's like court-appointed lawyers in that they're assigned to defend the poor. However, there are financial qualifications that must be met in order to be awarded a court-appointed lawyer; it is exclusive to the poor and unemployed. The borderline working poor, lower-middle class, middle class, and economically upward either have to pay for their lawyer or go without. A lawyer typically charges a minimum of $150 per hour. Bradford and the rest of the pro-government-worker bail crowd have no problem with this. They don't refer to lawyers as for-profit counsel. If they were consistent and really fighting for the lower income people, they would be calling for an end to for-profit legal counsel and demanding all lawyers be employed by the state. What is more burdensome to the family of the person who gets arrested, the $200 premium or the cost of the lawyer? Quoting further,

"The bail system works for people who are able to obtain release on recognizance and not so well for those who are not able to."[12]

This applies to government-worker bail as well. Does the pro-government-worker bail lobby really want to go there? How about "the entire judicial system works for people who can afford it but not so well for those who are not able to?" Recalling how a bail bond is executed in any of the four states where for-profit bail is banned, the defendant's family or friends must pay the entire 10 percent up front. There is no option for a payment plan. However, in states where for-profit bail exists, there are bondsmen who do not require the full premium up front in order to bond someone out of jail. Therefore, I submit that government-worker bail is more burdensome for the lower economic classes than for-profit bail. With all of the unjust procedures and processes being perpetrated by the state criminal justice system, it just seems to be a stretch to believe that the 10 percent bail bond premium is the big one to be corrected, especially when it's being presented inaccurately and falsely.

For-Profit Bail Bondsmen Are Not Criminal Justice Professionals

For this argument, Bradford starts off by claiming that the number of people arrested and booked has skyrocketed. However, he cites no evidence. Also, just because someone is arrested and booked doesn't mean a secured bail bond was issued. This is a sleight-of-hand technique to make a false implication without actually stating it. I believe the opposite is true, at least in the Central Virginia area. For example, the new Richmond City Jail opened in 2014. It was built with less capacity than the old jail. Richmond City's plan to deal with this was to issue fewer secured bonds. A *Richmond Times-Dispatch* article dated December 1, 2013 explained:

> Commonwealth's Attorney Michael N. Herring told the *Richmond Times-Dispatch* that he is now directing his prosecutors—when handling cases in which they normally would request a bond of less than $10,000—to instead ask a judge to release the defendant on his own word that he will return to court and stay out of trouble.[13]

Next, Bradford claims that for-profit bondsmen have no mechanism for determining *"the dangerousness as a factor in their decision to bond."* Accordingly, our only factor and guidance is the bond amount. First of all, Bradford failed to specify what is meant by *"dangerousness."* Is it that the person being released is a danger to society or a danger that the person will flee and skip court? Either way, this statement indicates the unserious nature of the government-worker bail argument. In Virginia, the magistrates and judges determine if there should be a bond and, if so, how much. One of the factors is the offense; another is the criminal history of the defendant. There are other factors as well. However, it is their job to determine if a defendant should be released while awaiting trial, not the bail bondsman. I have yet to hear of any bondsman who has bonded out a defendant accused of murder or rape.

As for bondsmen using only the bond amount to ascertain the risk, that assertion is absolutely wrong. I would wager a bondsman uses more *"mechanisms"* than government-worker bail agents. Examples include interviews with family and friends, criminal record, employment history, and family relationships. It can be the way someone answers a question that can determine the outcome of performing the bond. I've written $10,000 bonds I felt were safer than some $1,000 bonds.

Bradford also maintains, once again, that the for-profit bondsman is driven solely by the profit motive. I can say that in the several years I've been writing bonds, most bonding agents, myself included, derive satisfaction in helping people get through this legal process. We provide a service to people. While there may be some bondsmen who care only about the money, there are many who take pride in performing this service well. Isn't that the case for most any industry?

What Bradford fails to mention is that writing bad bail bonds is not profitable. Whenever a defendant skips, the immediate costs are paid by the bondsman, not the cosigner. The bondsman attempts to collect the costs from the cosigner; however, if the cosigner is unable or unwilling to pay, the expenses of fugitive recovery and bond forfeiture rest on the bondsman to pay. So following Bradford's logic, if bondsmen are solely motivated by profit, they should be more proficient in judging a safe bond from an unsafe bond.

Bail Bondsmen Don't Address Public Safety

There are a couple of points here that deserve refuting. First, Bradford claims "that most people who miss their court date are apprehended by law enforcement, not bail agents."[14]

But his reference for this is a single person from a district attorney's office in Lubbock, Texas. No study, no statistics, just that a guy from the DA's office said so. Here is some context:

When a defendant skips court, that person is a fugitive. This means that if law enforcement does come in contact with the fugitive, they will perform an arrest. But "come into contact" is the operative idea here. It can mean they get caught, by chance, from a routine traffic stop. Once a defendant decides to skip court, they typically leave their known residence. They move out and stay with friends or family. Usually neither the court, pretrial services, nor the police have the resources to actively pursue the fugitive.

According to the *Henrico Citizen* article "FIT to be served," dated May 12, 2015, there were 3,352 outstanding warrants in Henrico County. A portion of them were for failure-to-appear-in-court warrants and were actively pursued.

> According to Henrico Police Lt. Chris Eley, about half of those people are wanted on criminal charges. For the most part, the other half fall into one of three categories: failure to pay child support, traffic violations or failure to appear in court. . . .
>
> People legitimately forget that they have a court case, and the court issues a capias (an order to arrest) on them for not showing up. It might be six months later (that we pick them up) and they'll say, "Aww, I forgot all about that."[15]

If the fugitive is out on bond via a bail bondsman, it's in the bondsman's financial interest to get him or her back in jail. Bail bondsmen are like any other entrepreneur in that we try to reduce costs. (This is in sharp contrast to government agencies, like pretrial services.) What some bondsmen do for fugitive recovery, depending on the circumstances, is locate the fugitive and then call law enforcement. There have been other instances where the cosigner would inform the police of the fugitive's location, just to get off the bond and avoid having to pay the full amount. Neither of those scenarios would occur with pretrial services.

This is what Bradford's sole opinion source in Lubbock, Texas, has no way of knowing. How did law enforcement come to apprehend the fugitive? These statistics would be very difficult to accurately access, as this type of information is most often not recorded. Clearly, there's more to it than a single sound bite from a guy who works in a Texas DA's office.

The other point Bradford made was that bail bondsmen have no role to ensure the defendant remains law abiding. Yes, that's true. A bail bondsman provides a financial guarantee to the court that a defendant will appear at all future court dates related to the charges on the bond. That is the service we provide, and we do it better, more efficiently, and more cost effectively than any other alternative means, namely, pretrial services.

The question to be asked of Bradford is, "How does government-worker bail ensure the defendant remains law abiding?" The answer is they don't. There is no advantage government-worker bail has over for-profit bail regarding this. If the defendant is checking in with the pretrial services agent, that in no way precludes the defendant from committing another crime.

Unlike Bondsmen, Pretrial Services Agencies Measure Risk, Facilitate Services

Bradford's main point here is that government-worker bail provides many services, like drug testing and social service referrals, while for-profit bail does not. As stated before, this is an injustice to the defendant and should be stopped. It's definitely nothing to brag about. Bradford created a chart that summarized that for-profit bail bondsmen base their decisions only on the client's "ability to pay the bonding fee, assets available to pay full bail if FTA, and their subjective assessment," while the government-worker bail's decisions are based on the "number of prior FTAs, past convictions . . . , employment status, drug abuse status, and other information."[16]

This chart of Bradford's is so deceptive and wrong, it's difficult to know where to start. On the factual aspect of it, he sites no references nor backs up these assertions in any way. To claim that bail bondsmen don't look at prior FTAs, past convictions, drug abuse status, and "other information" is completely absurd. This one assertion calls into question the credibility of both Spike Bradford and the Justice Policy Institute.

His chart and assertions are also contradictory. He states that bail bondsmen base decisions on the client's ability to pay the bonding fee and the assets available to pay full bail if FTA, but not on their employment. Unless the client is independently wealthy, how is that possible? Wouldn't their employment be directly related to their ability to pay the fee and full bail?

Also in the chart is that government-worker bail takes into account their drug status while for-profit bail does not. One of the first lessons a bondsman comes to understand is that a hard-core drug addict is the riskiest bond to write. When someone has charges of "schedule I or II" drugs or larceny, it always requires further questions from a diligent bondsman.

Bail Bonding Is Not "Cheaper" than Pretrial Services

Bradford attempts to refute the fact that government-worker bail is much more expensive for the taxpayer than for-profit bail. His arguments against for-profit bail are wanting. First, he doesn't speak to real costs, but only "collateral" costs. What that really means is that the real costs for government-worker bail far exceed for-profit bail bonding. Government-worker bail requires the funding of an agency. The real taxpayer costs for this include employees, benefits, buildings, maintenance, etc. In Virginia, bail bondsmen are regulated by the Department of Criminal Justice Services (DCJS), but it's only part of what DCJS does. DCJS was not created, nor does it exist, solely to regulate bail bondsmen.

Regarding the collateral costs, his reasoning is, since many people are struggling financially, having them pay the 10 percent premium will cause them to become homeless.[17] This argument is so far-reaching that it's almost not worthy of refuting. However, I will refute it. First and most importantly, it's false. In the four states that have no commercial bail, the 10 percent must be paid before the defendant is released, so there's no advantage for government-worker bail over for-profit bail. Second, unlike the jails in the four states, most bondsmen do work with people regarding the 10 percent premium. This allows the loved one to get out of jail without paying the full bond premium upfront. Bradford's assumption, that people will pay the bondsman before paying for their rent or food, is laughable. In fact, if you were to ask a bondsman about this, the answer would be something like, "We're often the last one on the list to get paid."

So I'm very skeptical about the true agenda of the pro-pretrial lobby. There are elements and policies within the criminal justice system that do place an unfair burden on the lower economic classes. Posting bail is pretty low on the list. It seems like they're picking on the bail bonding industry because if the bail bonding industry were to cease to exist, their agencies would expand to fill the void. The bail bonding industry is in their way. They want to grow their agency, and it's truly a selfish motive cloaked in a deceptive argument that they're sticking up for the poor and helping people. Don't buy it!

Bradford's other argument about for-profit bail being more costly has to do with drug treatment. Government-worker bail performs drug treatment, while bail bondsmen do not. This argument recognizes that many drug cases fall into a dual mechanism of being bonded out with a bail bondsman and also reporting to pretrial services. He contends that once a defendant is placed under the supervision of pretrial services, there is no need for the bondsman, because the government workers will follow and ensure the defendant makes his or her court dates.[18] So there is no need for a bail bondsman, since pretrial services can do both.

I have the best solution to resolve this dual mechanism issue: totally remove this function from pretrial services. Fire pretrial services. The assumption that pretrial services can supervise and ensure the defendant will show up to court is a false premise. Just as bail bondsmen don't make people pee in a cup, pretrial services don't make defendant's show up to court; they simply issue another capias on the defendant for failure to show up to court. Bail bondsmen ensure the defendants show up to court and with no cost to the taxpayer.

For-Profit Bail Bonding Affects
Judicial Decisions around Release

The contention by the pro-government-worker bail is that a judge will alter the bond amount based on what bail bondsmen will charge, so the bond amount may be increased substantially. Following an example put forth by Bradford, say a judge deems the flight risk should be $5,000, so the bond should be set at $50,000 (given that most states mandate a minimum of 10 percent premium on bonds). But for states that have no minimum and it becomes common knowledge that defendants are being bonded out with a 2 percent premium, the bond will then be set at $250,000. There's just one problem with this, this entire argument is false and totally made up. To quote:

> The industry standard for bail bond premiums is ten percent of the full bail amount. Many states mandate a minimum bail percent for bond premiums, usually ten percent, **but others**

have no such restriction. This allows for-profit bondsmen to compete with each other and under-cut offers by other bail agents, charging as little as two percent of the bail.[19] [Emphasis added]

The "but others have no such restriction" is the operative phrase here and is a complete deception. Bradford failed to specify which states have no such restriction, and that's because there aren't any. The rates vary among states; for example, the bail bond cost in Virginia is a minimum of 10 percent and a maximum of 15 percent, while Nevada is 15 percent or $50, whichever is greater,[20] but there are no states that allow a 2 percent premium for bail bondsmen.

Bail Industry Has Influence in State Legislatures to Fight Government-Worker Bail

For several years, the bail bonding industry has been fighting the pretrial services lobby, trying to protect their industry in states across the nation. This is somehow seen as a negative, perhaps some type of corruptive influence, by the pro-government-worker bail advocates.

This is analogous to the typical schoolyard bully beating up on everyone until someone fights back and pops him in the nose. When that happens, the bully cries and whines about the person who fought back.

To abolish bail bondsmen, or compensated sureties, state laws are going to have to be changed. The NAPSA and other pretrial agencies are working to do just that. So am I to believe that it's OK for pretrial services agencies to participate in the political process to further their agenda of taking over the bail industry in order to grow their agencies, but it's not OK for the bail bonding industry to participate in the political process to protect their interests?

Therefore, this complaint that the bail industry is being somewhat underhanded by participating in the political process clearly shows the blind arrogance of Bradford and the pro-pretrial services lobby.

The NAPSA and other pretrial services agencies are the aggressors here. Their agenda is to grow their agencies. However, bail bondsmen are in their way. For any state to abolish bail bondsmen, their state and local pretrial services budget will have to grow to take on the extra workload that is currently being provided by bail bondsmen. It will be costly to the taxpayer. Also, those who are incarcerated, and their families, will be the ones who suffer the inefficiencies of being "processed" by another government agency. (They'll still have to pay the 10 percent, so the poor will not be better off.) In the end, those who are arrested, along with their families, will suffer a lower quality service, and the taxpayer will suffer a higher tax bill.

The For-Profit Bail Industry Is Ripe for Corruption

Bradford contends that the bail bond industry is just too corrupt and therefore should be abolished. However, his arguments are scattered and nonsensical. He first points out how the bail industry in the early 1900s in San Francisco was fraught with corruption and graft.

I have to concede these facts. It's generally accepted that the first commercial bondsmen in America were the McDonough brothers, who first worked as bartenders in their father's bar in San Francisco at the turn of the twentieth century. Lawyers would frequent their bar, and the brothers began putting up the bail money for the lawyers. They soon figured out it was more profitable to deal directly with the defendants. They built a network among themselves, the lawyers, the police, and the judges. There was total corruption and graft going on, and everyone was on the take. Note that all aspects of the criminal justice system were involved in this corruption. Bradford gave the judges, lawyers, and police a free pass while pinning it all on the bondsmen. Be that as it may, the bail bonding industry, admittedly, has a very seedy reputation. With that stated, we've come a long way since those days. While there are still issues involving bail bondsmen that could be improved, the reality rarely lives up to the caricature of the bail bondsman who also might ask something like, "Hey, buddy, wanna buy a watch?".

Getting back to Bradford's arguments, he concedes that many bondsmen are honest and truly care about their clients but that some are not. He lists the types of corruption charges: illegal bribing of justice officials and personnel, sex for bail, or brutal and terroristic tactics used to extort clients' friends and family.[21] I'll address each one of these.

Regarding illegal bribing of justice officials and personnel, there is no data to back this up. However, I have heard of this occurring in Virginia jails. Bondsmen have told me they're sure that some bondsmen make associations with either personnel at the jail or inmates at local jails. Whoever is on the take will make sure the person being bonded out lets the bondsman know who got them the bond. The bondsman will then pay off the inmate or staff member later. This is extremely difficult to prove and is therefore regarded as heresay.

In Virginia, the Department of Criminal Justice Services (DCJS) is charged to regulate bail bondsmen. They have the authority to investigate and stop the corrupt bondsmen from writing bonds by removing their license. The solution to this issue is that bondsmen, or anyone else who knows of this, should report it to DCJS. DCJS should then take swift action against the bondsmen, as well as any other participants involved.

As for the sex-for-bail issue, I devote a section of this book to that. I'll just say here that it's against the law, and any bondsman who entertains this payment option should have their license revoked and face the legal consequences.

His last corruption claim is that "brutal and terroristic tactics [are] used to extort clients' friends and family." There is nothing like overstating a case to make a point—badly. His argument for claiming bondsmen employ terrorist tactics is that bondsmen are given complete control over their client's liberty. This control is a "very toxic situation and one in which some bondsmen have succumbed to the lure of corruption."[22] Of course, there's no explanation of what that means or how he got to that conclusion.

Bottom Line

Many of the bondsmen I talk to believe pretrial services should be eliminated completely. Perhaps they are right, but I do think there should be a way for the indigent who pose no flight risk to get bail. However, Virginia and its citizens would be better off if pretrial services programs, laws, and budgets were at a minimum, largely curtailed.

Pretrial services implementation of putting defendants through pretrial probation is an affront to the ideals of our criminal justice system. The Virginia legislature should revisit the Pretrial Services Act (Virginia Code § 19.2-152.2 thru § 19.2-152.7) and, at a minimum, remove all but the very limited and defined role of attending to the indigent. No more drug testing, referrals to treatment or counseling, and, especially, no more issuing capiases. To mention a related aside, from time to time, I hear officials discuss the challenges of jail overcrowding. Typically, the ideas to alleviate it are to give fewer bonds and release inmates who don't pose a risk to society. How about this: Remove the stupid laws that force the police to have to make bogus arrests, like arresting someone for not showing up to a pretrial service's appointment or any other failure to comply to an unjust pretrial condition.

Regarding all of the criticisms of the bail industry by the Justice Policy Institute, authored by Spike Bradford, this book should give evidence that the arguments for eliminating the bail industry in favor of pretrial services are baseless, virtually made up, and serve only to further the agenda of the pretrial services agencies. Even if it is at the cost and detriment of the defendants they purportedly claim to help (which it is), it doesn't matter to the pretrial services lobby that is advancing this self-serving agenda.

Here is a truism that applies to this issue. If there are two opposing sides to an issue, and one side has to exaggerate, overstate their case, obfuscate, and rely on untruths, then their issue most certainly lacks substance, and there's an alternative motive behind it. If the cause is true, why would it have to be backed up by untruths and obfuscation? The answer is, it wouldn't. In this case, the ulterior motive for this is to grow the pretrial services agencies.

Also of note, I attempted to contact Bradford by email to clarify many of his arguments and have not received a response.

Chapter Eight

Virginia's Debtor's Prison: Surrender Your Driver's License

For debtors in early America, consequences were typically harsh. Many states dealt with debtors by imprisoning them in debtor's prisons until their debt was paid. The thinking was that once jailed, their family or some other interested party would pay their debts for their freedom. That would have had to be the only way, because, obviously, once the debtor is jailed, he or she would be unable to work to pay off the debt. This injurious practice was done away with by the mid-1800s.

However, Virginia has, unfortunately, instituted it with a different method. The state simply suspends driver's licenses when a citizen doesn't pay court costs, fees, or fines. For most people, the inability to drive means the inability to work and function. While the person may not physically be in jail, the state has just essentially stopped him or her from earning a living until their debt is paid off.

It is often devastating, if not life changing, to lose a license. For instance, many people have occupations that involve driving, so they automatically lose their job. Also, when a job applicant divulges that he or she has a suspended driver's license, that applicant is typically placed in the "unable to arrive at work reliably" pile. So, it's extremely difficult, if not impossible, to get a job.

As with almost any bad policy, the demographic hit the hardest by this is the poor and working poor. It's not as if they can just hire a driver to drive them to work or shuttle their kids. What usually happens is that they simply drive without a license and hope they don't get caught. Then, if they get pulled over, they can be 'cuffed and taken to jail for driving with a suspended license. They get more bail, court costs, and a fine, adding more to their debt. This is clearly a law to create criminals out of citizens who aren't criminals.

I recall one client I had. A twenty-five-year-old young woman called me just bawling because her lawyer told her she was going to need a bondsman the next day. She was going to court for a charge of driving without a license. Her license had been taken away for not paying a fine for a traffic ticket. Despite being a single mom of a three-year-old daughter with almost no family support, she had managed to become an LPN. She was especially upset for a couple of reasons. First, she was afraid for her daughter. She said she had no one to take care of her. I asked her if her parents could help by taking care of her daughter while she went to court. She said that they weren't in a position to help her. It ended up that the father of her daughter took care of the small child during her court date and incarceration. The other reason she was crying was that she was scared to go to jail. She had never been in trouble before. Her bond ended up being just $300. When I bonded her out, I remember her eyes were bloodshot from crying. She told me she had been bawling all day.

This was one of the first bonds I wrote. It seemed like a complete waste of resources to put this young woman through the system. This girl was working very hard trying to get by and raise her daughter and was not able to pay a traffic ticket. I'm not suggesting she should not have been required to pay the ticket, but this just seemed to be piling debt on her.

Shouldn't suspending or revoking someone's driver's license be reserved for those who are deemed a danger behind the wheel? I hear politicians and others chant "driving is a privilege, not a right." That might be true, but taking someone's driver's license away shouldn't be taken lightly. A person's livelihood may be taken away along with their driver's license.

The Virginia DMV can suspend a person's driver's license for many reasons. Among them are:

- failure to pay court fines and costs for convictions for motor-vehicle-related or non-motor-vehicle-related violations, and
- failure to pay jail fees.

Along with that, once all the fines and fees are paid, DMV charges a fee to reinstate the driver's license. It ranges from $145 up to $220, depending on the reason for the suspension or revocation.

So when did the state of Virginia start doing this? In March of 1971, House Delegate A. L. Philpott referred H. B. 196 to Committee:

A BILL to amend the Code of Virginia by adding a section numbered 46.1-423.3, so as to provide for the suspension of operators' or chauffeurs' licenses for the failure or refusal to pay fines incurred for violation of any motor vehicle laws.

It passed later that summer and was signed into law by then-Republican governor, Linwood Holton. (A bit of unrelated trivia here: Governor Holton's daughter, Anne, is married to former governor and current Virginia senator, Tim Kaine.)

I inquired at different governmental agencies as to what was done prior to this law to people who did not pay their fees and fines. No one knew exactly. What I gathered from this is the local jurisdictions would likely have chosen to send it to collections and/or prosecute delinquent debtors in civil court.

This brings up a couple of points. First, a reality of any business is that some people will not pay their bill. The recourse for the creditor is to take the debtor to civil court. If a legal judgment is made in a creditor's favor, the debtor either pays or their credit may be downgraded. This is the only thing a private individual or business can legally do to a person or business that doesn't pay their bill. No other damage or harm can be done to the debtor by the creditor. This is not the case with the state and local governments. If they're the creditor, they will take away the person's ability to function in society by suspending their driver's license, thereby sentencing them to live "off the grid" until their debt is paid. If I didn't know better, I would almost believe the state is purposely trying to create a permanent underclass.

The larger point to this is to question the kind of government we are living with and tolerating. We have allowed it to become increasingly oppressive. This type of consequence would not be tolerated if done by a private business or corporation. Imagine not paying the phone bill, and instead of the phone provider dropping your service, they make it so you can no longer get phone service from any provider until they are paid. That would not be tolerated. Shouldn't the government adhere to the same rules as the governed? After all the political rhetoric about standing up for the little guy and the poor, instituting and maintaining these types of laws is contradictory and dishonest. It's no wonder politicians are viewed so poorly by private citizens.

So I have a theory and a proposal. My theory is that after a certain amount of time, a debtor will give up trying to pay the debt, even if it means not being able to legally drive. I have had numerous clients who operate off the grid and haven't been able to legally drive for years. I recall one young woman who breeds purebred cats. She actually does pretty well. She has no bank accounts and all of her transactions are in cash.

I attempted to get information from the local city and county courts pertaining to delinquent debts. The information requested was the delinquent debts currently outstanding that were incurred two, three, four, and seven years ago. However, none of the courts or agencies could get that specific information. They were able to give me the delinquent debts for that year, but couldn't distinguish when the debts began. So for the record, on this subject, I don't have data to back up my theory and proposal. I would like to state up front that this is not fact but conjecture. I feel I have to make that known; otherwise, if I were to put it down as fact without any proof, the pretrial services lobby might get confused and think I was working for them and try to hire me to collaborate with Spike Bradford.

Anyhow, the premise of my theory is that people who are employed, paying taxes, and engaged with others in the community are more beneficial to society than people who are unemployed and live off the government. How this pertains to suspending driver's licenses is that it drastically inhibits people in the lower economic classes from advancing economically. Not only will people in this situation not be able to pay the court fees and fines, the state may very likely have to continue paying welfare payments for them. So it's economically detrimental to the local governments, to society, and to the individual to suspend driver's licenses for not paying fees and fines. This practice is immoral. I cannot think of any policy or law more injurious to the poor and working poor. The old grievance "it's a crime to be poor" comes to mind here.

My proposal is to repeal the law now. Let the local jurisdictions collect the fees and fines as they see fit. They may be able to garnish wages or negatively affect credit as motivation for payment. They may be able to come up with other ideas to motivate debtors to pay. The effect on the public of repealing this law would be more citizens eligible to legally work in the workforce. Basic opportunities that were previously closed to them would now be open.

Second, periodically, forgive the debts. As a jumping off point, how about every seventh year the local and state governments forgive all debts incurred by its citizens, at least eighteen months prior. The reason for the eighteen-month buffer is, suppose this is enacted and in October of the sixth year someone gets a speeding ticket. If he or she knows the fine will be forgiven in a couple of months, he or she might be inclined to wait it out and not pay it. However, it would be difficult to endure eighteen months or more of being a debtor to the local government, so he or she would likely just pay it.

A primary benefit of this would be that by cutting people a break and giving them a second chance, many of them would seize upon this and be motivated to work since they know they will be able to keep their earnings rather than just working for the local governments and the DMV. The other benefit is that people would have a better attitude toward their local governments. When people are directly affected in a positive manner by their local government, the attitudes will change. Imagine a person having a $700 bill to the court hanging over their head for two years and receiving a letter saying the $700 is forgiven; nothing is owed. Rather than having the attitude, of "The stinking greedy state is just going to take my money; they're keeping me down," their attitude would become, "Holy cow, I can't believe this. Maybe they're not so bad after all."

You might be thinking that if they are the poor or working poor, they still won't be paying much, if anything, in taxes. That's true, at least initially, and it may be for some time. But there can be only good to come from it. On the other side, I see no benefit to suspending driver's licenses based on inability to pay debts. The only motivation I can see for it is a sinister one. By putting up roadblocks to prevent upward economic mobility, it is easier for the government to control and influence the people.

I understand that this may be a radical idea, but I think it is a good one. However, I certainly cannot claim credit for it. It's actually from the Bible, Deuteronomy 15:1:

"At the end of every seven-year period you shall have a relaxation of debts."

Chapter Nine

Is Chesterfield Really Arrest-A-Field?

As a bail bondsman, I hear a lot of stories about the police, mostly from the arrestee side of the story. Bondsmen don't need to know the details of the arrest. We are not the lawyers. Whatever the defendant or their family chooses to divulge is completely voluntary. Sometimes they tell me nothing. Often they divulge some details with an attitude of contriteness. (Actually, I don't really see the contriteness attitude too much.) Other times, when someone feels they have been genuinely wronged, they come out defiant, telling me everything. For all of these, it should go without saying that I'm getting only half the story.

I have noticed two forms of the defiant defendant. The first is when the circumstance or some third party is at fault. This occurs often with domestic assault cases. For example:

"I got in an argument with my girlfriend and so her mom called the cops. That old bag lied and said I threatened to kill her, but I never did. That ugly witch just never liked me!"

They don't blame the officer who made the arrest, but some other factor.

The other is when they blame the officer for making the arrest in the first place. They are either totally innocent and the officer was too gung-ho to use any common sense to make the right judgment, or they admit they were technically breaking the law, but shouldn't

45

have gotten arrested, because there's no benefit to society in making the arrest. An example of this would be:

> I went to a party and knew I was going to drink, so I walked because it wasn't very far. I got drunk and walked home. I chilled and watched television for a couple of hours, then got hungry, so I drove my car to get some food. On my way back, a cop followed me as I neared my house. I pulled into my driveway and the cop came and talked to me. He made me blow, and I blew a .10. The cop's partner kept telling him to let this one go, but this Barney Fife cop arrested me. What a jerk.

This last one, where the arrested blames the officer and has a negative, as well as adversarial, opinion of the police, occurs in all jurisdictions. (As an aside, that was a real story from one of the persons I bonded out in Chesterfield.) However, from my perception, it seems to occur more in Chesterfield County, at least more so than in Richmond, Henrico, or Hanover. I hear so much bashing of the Chesterfield Police; Chesterfield is Arrest-A-Field.

So I decided to determine if there's a higher propensity to be arrested in Chesterfield County than in other Greater Richmond localities. Under the Freedom of Information Act (FOIA), I submitted requests to the police departments of Chesterfield, Henrico, Hanover, and Richmond for a six-month time frame. For the period of January 1, 2014 through June 30, 2014, I asked for (1) the number of traffic-related arrests, and (2) the number of non-traffic-related arrests.

Bear in mind that this is not intended to be a fully scientific analysis with a definitive end-all conclusion. Rather, it is a single snapshot of one six-month period just to get an idea of whether or not Chesterfield is excessively making arrests. The results are in the following table:

Number of Arrests – January 1, 2014 thru June 30, 2014

	Population (Projected Sept. 2014)	Density (Persons/ Sq. Mile)	Number of Traffic Arrests	Number of Nontraffic Arrests	Total Number of Arrests
Chesterfield	327,245	773	22,917 (7.00%)	10,655 (3.26%)	33,572 (10.26%)
Henrico	318,612	1,363	24,036 (7.54%)	8,739 (2.74%)	32,775 (10.29%)
City of Richmond	214,114	3,623	9,117 (4.26%)	5,255 (2.45%)	14,372 (6.71%)
Hanover	101,918	218	4,168 (4.08%)	2,945 (2.88%)	7,113 (6.98%)

This chart shows quite a difference between the localities. Looking at the raw numbers of arrests, Chesterfield had the most with 33,572 arrests for this six-month period. That averages out to about 186 arrests per day and 8 arrests per hour. About two-thirds of those arrests were traffic related. Next was Henrico with 32,775 arrests for the six-month time frame, which averages 182 arrests per day and about 7 arrests per hour. However, three quarters of these arrests were traffic related. Next was the City of Richmond with 14,372 arrests for the six months, which averages 79 arrests per day and just over 3 arrests per hour with about 63% of all these arrests being traffic related. Lastly, Hanover predictably had the fewest arrests with 7,113 for six months, which averages about 39 arrests per day and 1.6 arrests per hour. Almost 60% of those arrests were traffic related.

For more context, when looking at these numbers in terms of percentages based on population, there is a considerable difference between Henrico's and Chesterfield's arrest percentage, and Richmond's and Hanover's. Hanover is easy to understand; it's more rural. Crime is higher in more densely populated areas. Then what about Richmond? Shouldn't Richmond have a higher arrest rate than Chesterfield and Henrico? There are a couple of things to consider. First, looking at the data, the largest gap has to do with the number of traffic-related arrests. The traffic-related percentage difference between Richmond and the surrounding counties is close to double

(4.26% vs. 7.54% and 7.0%). For the non-traffic-related percentage, it's much closer (2.45% vs. 2.74% and 3.26%). Also, Henrico and Chesterfield are virtually identical with an arrest/population ratio of just over 10%. The City of Richmond comes in at 6.71%, and Hanover is just above that with 6.98%.

I don't think there is a simple, definitive answer for this, but there are a couple of theories. The first is that the City of Richmond has public transportation while the surrounding counties do not, so there are more residents driving in the counties. It follows that if fewer people are driving, then fewer traffic-related arrests will occur.

Drilling down deeper, what is the difference in registered vehicles between Richmond and surrounding counties? From FOIA information requested from the Virginia DMV to get the number of registered vehicles by county and city, the number of vehicles (confined to passenger vehicles, light-duty trucks, and motorcycles) shows the percentages become much closer. (DMV numbers are as of June 2014.)

	Number of Passenger Vehicles, Light-Duty Trucks, and Motorcycles	Population	Vehicles/Person
Chesterfield	287,151	327,245	0.88
Henrico	260,916	318,612	0.82
Hanover	101,784	101,330	1.00
Richmond	141,989	214,114	0.66

Simplifying this table:

There are 8.8 registered vehicles for every 10 people in Chesterfield;
There are 8.2 registered vehicles for every 10 people in Henrico;
There are 10 registered vehicles for every 10 people in Hanover;
There are 6.6 registered vehicles for every 10 people in Richmond.

Using Richmond as the baseline and factoring this into the previous table of traffic arrests, we get:

	Traffic Arrests, as a Percentage of Population	Difference in the Rate of Traffic-Related Arrests, as Compared to Richmond	Number of Vehicles Per Person	Difference in the Number of Vehicles Per Person, as Compared to Richmond
Chesterfield	7.00%	2.74%	.88	33%
Henrico	7.54%	3.29%	.82	24%
Hanover	4.08%	(.18%)	1.0	52%
Richmond	4.26%	-----	.66	---

This table shows that Chesterfield has a 33% higher rate of vehicle ownership than Richmond, Henrico is 24% more, and Hanover is 52% higher than Richmond. While it may be a stretch to conclude there's a definite correlation between vehicle ownership and traffic-related arrests, I don't think it's altogether irrelevant. If there are more vehicles and more drivers, is seems that would lead to more traffic-related arrests. The more context, the better, and it would seem incomplete to leave this aspect out of consideration. However, it may be anybody's guess as to what the impact of this factor actually is. For instance, residents of the greater Richmond area drive across county and city lines all the time (where some of them get arrested). Some may argue it has little impact while others may think otherwise.

Perhaps a more tangible thought to explain this disparity of the number of arrests in the City of Richmond and surrounding counties is that there's more violent, or hard, crime in Richmond. Therefore, the Richmond police spend more time responding to rapes, murders, burglaries, etc., while the surrounding counties' police departments make more arrests for minor, quality-of-life offenses. According to the FBI.gov website,[23, 24] the data seems to support this. The following table is from the FBI.gov website. It shows that Richmond had about one-third more violent crime than Chesterfield and 20% more than Henrico in 2013.

	COUNTY / CITY			
	Chesterfield	Hanover	Henrico	Richmond
Violent crime	398	93	586	1,327
Murder and nonnegligent manslaughter	9	1	13	37
Rape (revised definition)	74	13	32	43
Robbery	144	10	200	624
Aggravated assault	171	69	341	623
Property crime	6,316	1,006	7,708	8,704
Burglary	1,356	85	1,091	1,817
Larceny – theft	4,734	874	6,255	5,949
Motor vehicle theft	226	47	362	938
Arson	51	5	30	50
Totals	13,479	2,203	16,618	20,112

So after looking at the results of all this, I would have to conclude that Chesterfield is not out of the norm for making arrests. However, a case may be able to be made that the norm is too high. Maybe the real answer is "compared to what." At any rate, Chesterfield's arrest rate is no worse than Henrico's. While there is always room to improve in making fewer frivolous arrests, maybe the reason Chesterfield is called Arrest-A-Field is simply because Chesterfield is an easy rhyme with Arrest-A-Field. Henrico has no easy rhyme, and Arrest-Ico just has no ring to it.

Chapter Ten

Sex for Bail

I have personally had just one occurrence of a sex-for-bail-bond incident. And NO, I did not engage in a sex-for-bail transaction. Although everything turned out fine with this bond, it was, at least on paper, the bond from hell. This bond had everything that is to be avoided: a cosigner who is a felon and landed back in jail during the bond, the bailee living, at times, in a motel; and a family telling me she's not going to go to court.

The bond was $3,500. The cosigner, I'll call him Jake, said he was a friend of the woman in jail, whose charge was possession of Schedule I or II drugs (hard drugs). They could pay only half the premium. He had his own construction company. I didn't check this out prior to signing it. I decided to write the bond and meet Jake at the jail. While doing paperwork, it became evident he was more than a friend with the bailee, whom I'll call Sue. Sue was also a stripper at a local strip club. Jake indicated to me that Sue would pay me the remainder of the premium on Friday. As a courtesy, I also tell all my clients to call me if they need anything, like a ride to the jail if they get in a bind. I tell them I can't guarantee to give them a ride, but I'll try to find a way for them to get there. For example, I've had to call cabs for clients at the last minute so they don't miss court.

So anyway, I bonded Sue out on a Sunday evening. Her hearing date was set for the following Friday. As a courtesy, I typically call my clients a day or two before their court date. After talking to both Jake and Sue on Thursday, the day prior to her court date, it was clear that they had totally forgotten. They were thankful that I had called them and assured me Sue would be there.

Then, about 11:30 p.m. that same evening, Sue called me saying that she was in a bind and wanted to know if I could provide a ride for her. Any male bondsman who would allow himself to be alone with a female client is putting himself at risk. I told her I would try to find her a ride, or I could call a cab for her. Then the conversation took an unexpected turn. She was thinking I might be able to come by her place to talk before going to court.

"Well, um," started Sue, "I was thinking that maybe you could come a little early so we could discuss the payment I owe you."

"Oh shoot," I started, still not clued into what she was hinting at. "We don't need to be face to face, we can discuss that right now on the phone if you want."

Sue sounded a little frustrated by now with my denseness. She continued, though.

"Well, um, I was thinking that you could come by to pick me up earlier. And. Um. You know, we can discuss payment, you know. And maybe there could be some other way, you know, I could pay you. Something else. Just us. Face to face. Alone."

Well, I don't need to be hit in the head with a brick to get it. I was a bit taken aback by this; I didn't expect this at all. So after a few "ums," "ohs," and "I see." I gathered myself and gave her my reply.

"Well, look. I have to play it straight with this. So, I can't do it."

I felt a bit like a high school kid turning down an invitation to go to the prom. Even though what she was proposing to me could potentially have turned my life upside down, I kind of felt bad for rejecting her. So I avoided the insult by expressing how flattered I was by it (in a strange way).

"I will tell you, though, that you're a very good-looking girl. You're very pretty. You're twenty-six, but I'm almost fifty. So believe me when I tell you that I think you'd much rather pay me the money than have sex with me. I'm doing you a favor."

She did go on to say that I didn't look fifty and apologized and hoped she hadn't freaked me out too much.

That is not the end of the story with Sue though. While awaiting trial, Jake's family called me up and urged me to revoke the bond and put her back in jail. Claiming she was a drug-addicted whore who would definitely skip court, they really felt it best for Sue to not have contact with Jake. These are not the types of phone calls a bondsman is eager to get. One thing that immediately came into my mind was that I'm sure glad I didn't barter with her. Imagine me attempting to revoke her bond but then hearing her say something like, "How about I talk to my lawyer to see what I can do to you about your method of payment." What a nightmare that could have been. Anyway, after some discussions with Sue (over the phone), I resolved that I would just keep a tighter leash on her but would not revoke the bond. This tighter leash was in the form of her contacting me relatively frequently. Besides, she still owed me the remainder of the premium.

It took her several weeks to pay me. During one of our phone conversations to arrange payment, she told me that she had spent the better part of the afternoon in a Health First clinic. She had gotten a call from someone she had had sex with who told her he had chlamydia. It turned out she didn't have it, but that was further validation to me that I made the right decision.

What's more, sometime later when I spoke to her, she was very distressed. She told me she was pregnant. Wow! Did I ever make the right decision by not taking a bite from that piece of fruit! I can't even imagine having to deal with a possible STD and an illegitimate pregnancy. Had I taken the bait, not only could it have ended my bail bonding business, but it also could have had a devastating effect on my personal life.

While I do joke about it, it is really a serious circumstance that bail bonding men and women may have to deal with from time to time. Aside from the illegality and immorality of it, the encounter emphasized how stupid it is to have sex with clients. Even if, under the best scenario, she never brought it up or ever told anyone, I would have known and would have had to continue to look over my shoulder for a very long time.

Chapter Eleven

Inmates Are Revenue Generators

It costs money to house inmates. Local jurisdictions pay for this primarily through local and state taxes. There are also charges to the inmates and their families for some of these costs, which is only fair. However, there's a difference between getting some compensation from the inmates, and gouging and exploiting them. Regarding the phone system and how inmates make calls, this falls easily into the category of exploitation.

The vendor for the inmate phone systems for most, if not all, of Virginia jails is Global Tel-Link (GTL). After performing a cursory look at the reviews for this company, the impression is that GTL is a completely unscrupulous company. A few of the common complaints are:

They have been ripping me off for months! Lying about who's charging the extra fees taken off my account, blaming the phones in jail/prison for the dropped calls, refusing to do anything about or refund calls, and a lot more!
Jennifer of Indianapolis, IN on May 23, 2015

I have been charged collect rates at $3.40 plus tax for more than 120 calls that should have been billed at $3.15 plus tax per NCDPS government website. I have been charged a $4.75 service fee eighteen times, but $7.95 six times. I have been *charged the full (yet incorrect) price for seven calls that had GTL technical problems, including a two-second call that was a busy signal. I have been told by GTL that my billing will not be researched and that I will never, ever receive any credit to my account.*

Elizabeth of New Bern, NC on May 14, 2015

I've been using Global Tel-Link for about a month to get calls on my cell phone from my fiancée. The costs of each call is $2.50 per phone call and the phone calls are fifteen minutes long. I only add money via Western Union which is a $10.95 sending fee. Talk about expensive.

Shabby, on March 7, 2011

There is no shortage of complaints for this company, and I have experienced the same thing. When I first started my business, I opened an account with forty dollars to receive phone calls. I have no idea what happened to that. I never received any collect phone calls from a jail. I recall I did attempt to contact the company but was unable to talk to anyone. At that point I decided I would no longer accept collect calls from jails.

Every now and then when I bond someone out, the family members will ask if I can get the message to their loved one in jail that they're working on getting him or her out, but to please stop making phone calls to them because it costs a small fortune. After getting several of these types of comments, I looked into it. What I have concluded is that exploitation and overt theft are being waged against the inmates, or specifically their families and friends. I don't know how anyone can defend this. Oh, and by the way, bondsmen are unable to get any messages to inmates at any of the jails.

The main perpetrator of this is GTL. I have attempted to find all of the hidden charges for the GTL phone calls, but it is not easy and is quite complicated. However, an organization called the Prison Policy Initiative (PPI) has performed extensive research on this topic. Their works on this topic include, "The Price to Call Home: State-Sanctioned Monopolization in the Prison Phone Industry"[25] and "Please Deposit All of Your Money: Kickbacks, Rates, and Hidden Fees in the Jail Phone Industry."[26] In the latter article, PPI details these exorbitant rates and explains why they've come about:

> Several unique and deliberate features of the prison phone industry lead to these prices. First, each prison system or local jail enters into an exclusive contract with a telephone company, granting that telephone company a monopoly in the state prisons or at the local jail. Second, in all but a few locations, the telephone companies are contractually obligated to pay back to the correctional facility a large portion of the revenue collected, thereby increasing the per-minute calling rates. Such kickbacks are known as "commissions." Third, in order to collect revenue to make up the money lost to commissions, prison telephone companies add hefty charges through multitudes of extra fees that often nearly double the price of a call. These fees—the vast majority of which do not exist in the ordinary telephone market—drive the telephone bills charged to people with incarcerated loved ones to astronomical levels.[27]

To summarize, GTL is awarded the contract, not based on quality of service or anything of that nature, but rather on how much money the jail or local government, will receive in the form of kickbacks. Then GTL piles on fees that go into their pockets to offset the commissions it has to pay.

There is an important aspect that should first be understood that pertains to who actually decides to employ GTL with these egregious practices. Local sheriff's departments run the jails. However, that does not mean the sheriff decides policy for the jails. While local governments differ in how this is managed and who makes the decisions, the sheriff's department is often not the decision maker in this at all.

Take, for example, the City of Richmond Justice Center (that's the name of the Richmond jail). These decisions fall under the City of Richmond governing bodies (city council, etc.). This decision comes specifically from the Richmond City's procurement department. But the point here is that the sheriff or the sheriff's department has nothing to do with it, so don't blame them. In fact, all of the revenues generated from the phone calls go into the City's general operating budget. Neither the jail nor the sheriff's department receives a penny of the revenues, at least directly. By the way, how much money does the City of Richmond get from this? In fiscal year 2014, the revenues generated from inmate phone calls for the City of Richmond was $372,932. (For the Chesterfield jail, it was $68,145.31.)

There are a few points to bear in mind here. First, it would be a fallacy to think this money is being taken from the inmates. Actually, it is being taken from the inmates' families. Second, this number, $372,932, is just the commissions received by the City of Richmond. It is the kickback from the charges of the minutes from the inmates' phone usage. The inmates' families also had to pay for GTL's portion on top of that, as well as all of the exorbitant fees GTL charges. I was unable to find that number, but would it be safe to assume the money extracted from the families would be double Richmond City's take? Triple maybe?

Lastly, it may be easy for law-abiding citizens to have the opinion that "well, they shouldn't have committed the crime." However, many of the inmates in jails have not been found guilty but are simply awaiting trial. Many citizens have the idea that the inmates are typically murderers, rapists, drug dealers, burglars, and others who commit violent or actual criminal behavior against their fellow citizens. But the reality is that many of the inmates are in jail for offenses such as driving without a license, trespassing, drug usage, and other nonviolent, "victimless" offenses. Even if that were not the case and every one of the inmates had committed a violent or dangerous criminal act, would it still be OK to shake down the inmates' families for this?

Again, there is nothing wrong with getting a reimbursement from the inmates and their families for the phone service used. But this is not what is being done. This is a legalized shakedown of the inmates' families and should be stopped.

Conclusion

Thanks for reading this, and I hope you found it informative and interesting.

For most of the topics raised in this book, an entire book could be devoted to each. Also, each one of these topics may be just the tip of the iceberg for other issues. For example, could there be other ways policies are set up for inmates to generate revenue? What about purchasing supplies for inmates, or video conferencing with family members, etc.?

At any rate, hopefully some of these issues will be addressed and improved upon; but it is up to the citizens of our state to put pressure on their governments to do so.

Notes

1. "History of Bail and Pretrial Release," T. Schnacke, M. Jones, and C. Brooker. Updated September 24, 2010, Pretrial Justice Institute. http://www.pretrial.org/download/pji-reports/PJI-History%20of%20 Bail%20Revised.pdf.

2. "Comprehensive Community Corrections Act and Pretrial Services Act: Alternative Funding Methodology Feasibility Report." October 2000, Virginia Department of Criminal Justice Services. http://www.dcjs.virginia.gov/corrections/pretrial/fundingformula.pdf.

3. "Report on the Comprehensive Community Corrections Act for Local-Responsible Offenders and Pretrial Services Act, July 1, 2012–June 30, 2013." January 2014, Virginia Department of Criminal Justice Services. http://www.dcjs.virginia.gov/corrections/pretrial/FY2012-2013_CCCA_webpdf.

4. "For Better or for Profit: How the Bail Bonding Industry Stands in the Way of Fair and Effective Pretrial Justice," S. Bradford. September 2012, Justice Policy Institute. http://www.justicepolicy.org/uploads /justicepolicy/documents/_for_better_or_for_profit_.pdf.

5. "Panel would scrap bail money system," M. Dresser. November 15, 2013, *Baltimore Sun*. http://articles.baltimoresun.com/2013-11-15 /news/bs-md-bail-eliminate-20131115_1_bail-bondsmen-task-force-bail-hearings.

6. *NAPSA Standards on Pretrial Release*, third edition. National Association of Pretrial Services Agencies. https://www.dcjs.virginia.gov /corrections/pretrial/napsaStandards2004.Pdf.

7. "Probation FAQ." Accessed October 18, 2015, FindLaw. http://criminal.findlaw.com/criminal-procedure/probation-faq.html.

8. "About," Accessed October 18, 2015, Justice Policy Institute. http://www.justicepolicy.org/About1.html.

9. "For Better or for Profit".

10. Ibid., page 13.

11. Ibid., page 14.

12. Ibid., page 16.

13. "Prosecutor's plan tackles overcrowding," R. Williams. October 25, 2013. *Richmond Times-Dispatch.* http://www.richmond.com/news /prosecutor-s-plan-tackles-overcrowding/article_56cab4cd-3a29- 56d0-b31d-942d39374b11.html?-mode=jqm.

14. "For Better or for Profit," page 1.

15. "FIT to be served," R. McKinnon. May 12, 2015. *Henrico Citizen.* http://www.henricocitizen.com/news/article/fit_to_be_served0512# .VhuYZflViko.

16. "For Better or for Profit," page 2.

17. Ibid.

18. Ibid., pages 20–21.

19. Ibid., page 2.

20. Nevada Revised Statutes. Accessed October 18, 2015. http://www.leg.state.nv.us/nrs/NRS-697.html#NRS697Sec300.

21. "For Better or for Profit," page 40.

22. Ibid., page 4.

23. "Crime in the United States 2013, Table 10," FBI, Criminal Justice Information Services Division. Accessed October 19, 2015. http://www.fbi.gov/about-us/cjis/ucr/crime-in-the-u.s/2013/crimein-the-u.s.-2013/tables/table-10/table-10-pieces/table_10_offenses_known_to_law_enforcement_by_virginia_by_metropolitan_and_nonmetropolitan_counties_2013.xls.

24. "Crime in the United States 2013, Table 8," FBI, Criminal Justice Information Services Division. Accessed October 19, 2015. http://www.fbi.gov/about-us/cjis/ucr/crime-in-the-u.s/2013/crimein-the-u.s.-2013/tables/table-8/table-8-state-cuts/table_8_offenses_known_to_law_enforcement_virginia_by_city_2013.xls.

25. "The Price to Call Home: State-Sanctioned Monopolization in the Prison Phone Industry," D. Kukorowski. September 11, 2012, Prison Policy Initiative. http://www.prisonpolicy.org/phones/report.html.

26. "Please Deposit All of Your Money," D. Kukorowski, P. Wagner, and L. Sakala. May 8, 2013, Prison Policy Initiative. http://www.prisonpolicy.org/phones/pleasedeposit.html.

27. Ibid., Endnotes. http://www.prisonpolicy.org/phones/pleasedeposit.html#_ftn10.